# Ceal Floyer

**IKON**

Ceal Floyer

# Foreword

This is the most comprehensive exhibition to date of work by Ceal Floyer. Involving video, sound and light projection, works on paper and sculptural pieces based on readymade objects, it embodies a subtle minimalism.

Floyer's work is informed by a very particular sense of humour, derived from shifting points of view, double-takes and an idiosyncratic reordering of everyday phenomena. It communicates simultaneously the vital possibility of creativity in any situation and a constant hint of absurdity.

Floyer's *Ink on Paper*, a new version of a series made especially for this exhibition, involves the complete draining of felt-tip pens into sheets of blotting paper. Circles of colour grow imperceptibly as a pen is held in the centre of a sheet. The result overall – a systematic series of circles, across the colour spectrum made from a whole new set of pens – is visually compelling.

Such fusion of process and finished work occurs often in Floyer's artistic practice and this is epitomised by one of her earliest works, *Light Switch*, 1992. Here a slide projector beams the actual-size image of a light-switch directly onto a wall. Any illusionism is undermined by the closeness of the image and its source; the image is obviously projected. At the same time Floyer suggests an inversion – a "switch" – of the cause and effect of electric light.

Typically, with deceptive simplicity, Ceal Floyer implies a whole range of other ways in which the world might work. This is something which the best art has to offer, and is a fundamental motivation of Ikon's artistic programme.

We would like to take this opportunity to thank especially The Henry Moore Foundation for its generous support. The broadminded collaboration of the City of Birmingham Symphony Orchestra too, towards the realisation of *Nail Biting Performance*, is very much appreciated. Also thanks to Nicholas Logsdail and Lisa Rosendahl, at Lisson Gallery, for invaluable assistance in the preparation of this exhibition. Above all, we are immensely grateful to the artist for her rare and intelligent sensibility.

Jonathan Watkins
Director

**Half Empty**   1999
Colour photograph
on aluminium
120 x 120cm

# Have Trojan Horse, will travel

**A conversation between Jonathan Watkins and Ceal Floyer**

**JW** Often in your work you invert the assumed relationship between viewer and the subject, or the subject and its environment. You radically shift the point of view.

**CF** It's a way of apprehending the subject. In being taken to an extremely rational conclusion it often ends up turning itself inside-out at the last minute, making itself quite absurd, despite a concerted effort to make sense of a very simple phenomenon. There's something almost Sisyphean in my attempts to prove that something is really there, when there was no question about it in the first place. It's like mentioning the obvious but in a different tone of voice.

**JW** By aspiring to such rationality, are you attempting to eliminate a personal point of view, to suppress subjectivity?

**CF** The more pared down an idea or its presentation, as is quite characteristic of the work I make, the more I think it can apply to another train of thought. There's more chance of its coinciding with something in the real world – not *my* world, but *the* world. But this certainly makes it no less specific to me.

**JW** And your use of language, whether or not it is articulated, is crucial. Language is such a vital context of your work, I think, informing its meaning – so that even if the work is self-contained it's not hermetic. The potential verbalisation of the experience of a work of art or, equally, an everyday object, such as a garbage bag or a light switch, often provides a key to the effectiveness of your work.

**CF** It's important to me that the methods and technologies I use are relatively familiar to an audience – a sense of vernacular provides a suitable foil, or vehicle, that can liberate all sorts of conceptual activity. For me, the use of language, or rather *words*, is much more than a context; it's the same as the use any other material.

Interestingly, I think that language can both enhance and 'gazump' the potential meaning, or reading, of things. *Ink on Paper*, for example, acts as both the title of a series of drawings and a description of the process. I literally rest felt-tip pens on pieces of blotting paper and let what happens happen until they run dry. The result is something actually quite beautiful (which at first I found slightly alarming) and for me this is OK because it manages to stay faithful to the conceptual origins of the work.

**JW** And there's a more fundamental existential proposition being made, not unlike that found in the work of Fischli and Weiss, something along the lines of "here I am, with these things in this place, now what do I do?" It amounts, perhaps, to an assertion of the value of inventiveness.

**CF** But inventiveness surely arises from a discrepancy, or slippage, between an activity and its object, whatever that may be. In a way, that's what I meant about proving the existence of something that is indisputably already there. I suspect that the object generates the activity and not the other way around. And often, you know, I think that what informs my practice is a certain dissatisfaction with being an artist, with operating in this art context, even if it is the very situation that accommodates, and tolerates, my sort of cultural practice. I still don't trust it though. It's that Russian Doll syndrome. By admitting this scepticism I make myself vulnerable, and then, by manifesting this uncertainty as art, I compound the situation still further. It's a bit like being in a really loud and crowded room, a party, say, and suddenly the music stops and you're the last one left talking, and your words just sort of hang there in the air. Often the art world seems like a place where the ambient noise has been removed, the background airbrushed out.

**JW** This is particularly pertinent to your use of readymades. These objects, not originally destined for the art world, not made to receive such attention, become isolated and extremely scrutinised.

**CF** … and the same applies to ideas, familiar ideas, figures of speech and in fact language generally. I often feel that my ideas could be equally suited to a different professional context, but then doomed to end up as art.

**JW** Your work has so many references to the non-art world. It is as accessible as it is "tautological", as generous as it is economical.

**CF**  There's a fine line between something making poetic sense of itself and becoming a short circuit; saying nothing outside of itself. I still think the more defined or simple something might be in terms of content, the more space it opens up for thought and imagination. I want the manifestation of my ideas to be life-sized, not only regarding their scale, but also in terms of their relevance to their situation or medium. Then they're more like the ideas *behind* something. Art is just a manifestation, a Trojan Horse, for ideas.

**JW**  As you continue to consider the possibility of making a break with your identity as an artist, to escape from art, I wonder how this might be reflected in the development of your work. There seems to be such continuity in your career as an artist, nothing suggests itself as to what might constitute an early or a later work. There is a strong thread of interest in illusionism, and double-take, throughout.

**CF**  I have always found it strange to have my work referred to in terms of illusion, trickery or *trompe-l'oeil*. After all, what is a photograph or a projection of a photographic image or a sound recording if it's not illusory. I have always enjoyed working with the tension between the cause and effect of representation, which accounts for the blatant presence of the mechanism, or hardware, in my work.

**JW**  It dispels any illusion of illusionism.

**CF**  Exactly. It's very deliberate. In *Downpour*, the cropped framing and tilting of the image [in order to achieve the vertical lines of rainfall] is the decisive factor – that's why the work was made. The post-production phase was in mind throughout the whole process of filming.

Again on the subject of illusion, if someone wants to be tricked into perceiving something that's not there they will be. If they want to see a snowdrift in a sheet of white paper they will. It's a matter of hermeneutics, and similarly occurs within the distinctions between figuration and abstraction. Video and sound are particularly interesting to me in this respect since they offer the possibility of time-based revelation; a sort of cognitive and perceptual night-vision. *Blind*, for example, appears at first glance to be some kind of homage to the structural-materialist filmmaking of the 60s and 70s, or else just a rewinding video – gradually though it becomes obvious that it is an image *of* something, [a roller blind in front of a casement window], and so breaks out of its short circuit.

**JW**  The word "blind" of course also refers to the fact that the viewer can't see the blind until a breeze sucks it towards the window, and then we see the silhouette of the metal frame.

**CF**  Yes, "blind" is used both as a noun and as an adjective. The piece operates retrospectively, the periods of apparent sensory deprivation sporadically interrupted by the image of the object sharing its name. Similarly, with *Light*, I wanted the title simultaneously to name the subject of the work and the way it was being produced.

**JW**  Like the word "switch" in *Light Switch*, a work in which the relationship between cause and effect appears to be reversed. Your titles are another way of framing, like the video monitor, like the gallery, the dedicated art space, which determines much of the identity and meaning of a work of art.

**CF**  *Door* and *Garbage Bag*, like many of my titles in fact, are meant as an index, a way of undermining any false promises. *Door*, in its name at least, at no point alludes to any light emanating from *under* a door – it's the door itself that is being emphasised. Neither is *Garbage Bag* ever referred to as a bag-of-garbage. And, yes, the notion of "framing" is absolutely crucial to me. Naturally, the gallery, or whatever viewing situation, is its own big frame; a four-dimensional one as things are experienced through time … five-dimensional even, if you take into account the retrospective fall-out, the conceptual "afterimage". Much of the thinking behind what I do is derived from my experience of this situation. Throughout my time at art college when I worked part-time as a gallery invigilator at the ICA [London] I watched a lot of art being seen. And a lot of art being not seen. That was a training in itself. I discovered that presumption is a medium in its own right.

**JW**  People visiting a gallery (often) expect to see something enhanced or heightened, literal or metaphorically, in the spotlight. The formal modesty of your work, the fact that it is "life-sized", corresponds to your interest in what lies outside the presumed visual field; those things that nobody else is looking at. Your debut here of the *Nail Biting Performance*, biting your fingernails on stage between performances of a Beethoven overture and Stravinsky's *Rite of Spring* epitomises this tendency in your work.

At once this work is unassuming, time-based and choreographed. It is extremely site-specific and self-referential – "short-circuiting" – and absolutely engaging as it embodies the intense anxiety often felt by a performer prior to going onstage. It is an off-stage phenomenon, and it's not an illusion. Not only does it communicate an emotional state familiar both to members of the orchestra and the audience, it is also expressing your feelings as they actually occur.

**CF**   I've never bitten my nails live on stage before! And this work, performance, whatever it is – ultimately a live sound-piece – will depict the behaviour that signifies insecurity, and as you say, *pre*-performance nerves. It'll be the first time I've been physically present in my work – this fact alone will probably induce the very reaction which is its subject.

**JW**   Paradoxically, you have to be very visible.

**CF**   Initially I really didn't want it to be me myself at all onstage doing this thing, but somehow the idea of directing a performer to do it seemed not only extraneous – a vaguely baroque solution – but, ultimately, and ironically I suppose, a little bit pompous or egotistical.

In this case the context is a kind of plinth, and so it's back to art objects – and a readymade! But again, I'm dealing with the dead time between things, being a human entr'acte. It seems appropriate to personify the blind-spot between events. To shine a strong light into this space makes it somehow concrete.

**JW**   Such an event is strengthened by the fact that everything goes quiet when you walk on stage.

**CF**   It's strangely prophetic isn't it?

**JW**   And like the crowded room, the analogy for the art-world you were describing earlier…

**CF**   Yes.

overleaf:
**Door**   1995
35mm metal mask slide projection

**Untitled (Twin Decks)**   1999
Vinyl records, turntables and sound system

# Just Like That

**Jeremy Millar**

A woman walks into a bar, goes up to the barman, and asks him for
a *double entendre*. So he gives her one.

as told by Ceal Floyer

Ceal Floyer's work often seems like a joke, funnily enough. At first we may simply recognise a classically minimalist aesthetic, itself simple, elegant, perhaps somewhat dry; it may not coincide with our idea of the humourous, which often seems dependent upon a certain excess. Perhaps they resemble a form of pun, then, rather than jokes as such, a playing with words, with their materiality, where the pleasure lies in the play itself rather than a punch-line resolution. It seems clear, I think, that word-play is central to Floyer's work, as both a generative and an interpretative force (although maybe we shouldn't emphasise the before-and-after of so circular a working process). Let us take one of Floyer's more well-known works as an example.

*Light Switch* (1992) consists of a 35mm projection (that is, an image projected from a 35mm slide) upon a wall in a somewhat darkened room; also listed as part of the work is the plinth upon which the projector sits. The image projected upon the wall, near the door, is of a standard light switch. Of course, it is also a switch made of light, the title's other meaning. Indeed, to the list of materials which make up this work perhaps we should add the title itself, as this too is material from which the work is made. Indeed, it is the title, and the inherent ambiguity of the words of which it consists, which to a large extent determines the form of the work, which has given the circumstances in which the work might come about. The words do not simply name what is there (as if that is ever simple) but actually enable what is there to be there. It is the space for play within the words ("tropological space" Foucault called it) which allows the space for play between the image and that of which it is an image. The words make pictures.

I think that we might recognise a similar process echoed in the work of another artist, that of Raymond Roussel. That Floyer has never, to my knowledge, acknowledged

**Light Switch**   1992
35mm slide projection

Roussel as an influence is not surprising, given his relative obscurity in the English-speaking world (he is hardly famous in France, where at least the wordplay is in its original language). However, that does not mean that his influence has not found its way into her work by other means. Perhaps the most important artist (certainly in this context) who has acknowledged his debt to Roussel is Marcel Duchamp. "It was fundamentally Roussel who was responsible for my glass, *La Mariée mise à nu par ses célibataires, même* (*The Bride Stripped Bare by Her Bachelors, Even* 1915–23)" he commented in a 1946 interview. "Roussel showed me the way."[1] The wordplay of Roussel echoes throughout Duchamp's work, especially his *Large Glass* (indeed, any serious understanding of Duchamp's work is impossible without reference to Roussel). No doubt it also influenced Duchamp's own "morceaux moisis", or "wrotten writtens", such as the name of his female alter ego, Rrose Sélavy (Eros, C'est la vie, a phrase which he appropriated from Robert Desnos, himself an ardent supporter of Roussel), "Abominable abdominal furs", or the title of his 1926 collaborative film *Anémic Cinéma*, all of which might themselves be subject to Floyer's notion of "opening up a can of words".[2] Indeed, Michel Foucault's comments upon Roussel's work might usefully apply to Duchamp and Floyer also:

"In the reading, his works promise nothing. There's only an inner awareness that by reading the words, so smooth and aligned, we are exposed to the allayed danger of reading other words which are both different and the same. His work as a whole à systematically imposes a formless anxiety, diverging and yet centrifugal, directed not towards the most withheld secrets but toward the imitation and the transmutation of the most visible forms: each word at the same time energized and drained, filled and emptied by the possibility of there being yet another meaning, this one or that one, or neither one nor the other, but a third, or none."[3]

The importance, more generally, of Duchamp's work to any contemporary conceptual practice, such as Floyer's, need hardly be stated (although it could hardly be overstated).

Raymond Roussel was born in Paris in 1877, the son of an extremely wealthy stock-broker and property speculator. At the age of nineteen he underwent an intense psychological crisis, which he later described to the eminent psychologist (and teacher of Jung) Pierre Janet who was treating him:

"You feel something special when creating a masterpiece, that you are a prodigy… I was the equal of Dante and Shakespeare… Everything I wrote was surrounded in rays of light; I would close the curtains for fear the shining rays that were emanating from my pen would escape through the smallest chink; I wanted to throw back the screen and suddenly light up the world."[4]

The book which Roussel was writing at the time, *La Doublure* (1897), is a super-realist 5,600 line poem of the failings of a theatrical understudy, who when called to take the stage fumbles his actions and fluffs his lines. Alain Robbe-Grillet, the primary writer and theorist of the *nouveau roman* in the 1950s, wrote of the unsettling descriptive methods of Roussel's work (and perhaps we might let these words echo around our heads after we have finished reading them, as we look at Floyer's works):

"Empty enigmas, time standing still, signs that refuse to be significant, gigantic enlargements of minute details, tales that turn in on themselves, we are in a *flat* and *discontinuous* universe where everything refers only to itself. A universe of fixity, of repetition, of absolute clarity, which enchants and discourages the explorer...."[5]

Roussel published the work at his own expense and received only two reviews. The first described it as "more or less unintelligible", the second "very boring". As Roussel himself remarked, the book "plummeted to earth from the prodigious heights of glory". The author scarcely recovered from the fall.

The book which would help confirm Roussel's status as one of the most influential artists of the twentieth century was a work about his own works. Published two years after the author's death (by his own hand, in a hotel in Palermo in 1933) *Comment j'ai é'crit certains de mes livres (How I Wrote Certain of my Books)* sets out the various methods and procedures by which the author created the extraordinary scenes in works such as his novels *Impressions d'Afrique (Impressions of Africa*, 1910) and Locus Solus (1914), and the incredible complexity of his poem *Nouvelles Impressions d'Afrique (New Impressions of Africa*, 1932). "I have always intended to explain the way in which I wrote certain of my books", he writes at the beginning. "It involved a very special method [*procédé*]. And it seems to me that it is my duty to reveal this method, for I have the sense that writers in the future may perhaps be able to exploit it fruitfully."[6]

As in Floyer's work, it is the pun which lies at the heart of Roussel's creative process. He provides a famous example of his *procédé* from the story 'Parmi les Noirs', written when the author was in his early twenties. Like other stories written at around the same time, such as 'Chiquenaude' and 'Nanon', 'Parmi les Noirs' begins and ends with phrases which are identical except for a single letter; however, each main word has a different meaning from its mirror image at the other end of the work. So, 'Parmi les Noirs' begins: "Les lettres du blanc sur les bandes du vieux billard" (The letters [as of the alphabet] in white [chalk] on the cushions of the old billiard table), and finishes: "les lettres du blanc sur les bandes du vieux pillard" (the letters [correspondence] sent by the white man about the hordes of the old plunderer). As Roussel remarked, with these two phrases found, it was then a question of writing the narrative which would bring them together.

The *procédé* was developed to create yet more bizarre effects, as words, even syllables, were split and reflected darkly, simple phrases becoming metamorphosised into a whalebone statue which moves along rails made of calves' marrow, or the aerial pile-driver which creates a mosaic from human teeth. All written images and objects are, literally, made from words; however, with Roussel, they are only made possible through words, can only exist in the space which words create.

Floyer's work also raises some important – and related – points regarding the notion of imitation within art. As a concept it is familiar to most people, whatever their familiarity with Plato's *Republic* or Aristotle's *Poetics*. We look through art, as if through a transparent pane of glass, onto the thing itself, the "goodness" of the imitation dependent upon its likeness to that of which it is an imitation. So, thinking back to *Light Switch*, this would seem to qualify as a good imitation; it certainly looks like a light switch as opposed, say, to bowl of grapes or an Italian prince. Indeed, given the fact of its photographic reproduction it achieves a degree of verisimilitude which would have been almost inconceivable to the painters of Ancient Greece. However I think that we should consider it, and indeed a number of Floyer's works, as something similar but different in a number of important ways, that is, as an impersonation.

It might be interesting to return to Roussel and Duchamp when considering the notion of artistic impersonation. Roussel, for example, was himself a skilled impersonator. Michel Leiris learned from Roussel's companion Charlotte Dufrène that he "worked for seven years on each of his imitations, preparing them when he was alone, repeating phrases aloud to catch the exact intonation and copying gestures, and would end up achieving an absolute resemblance."[7] Indeed, it is certainly no accident that at the very end of *Comment j'ai écrit certains de mes livres*, just before he hopes for "a little posthumous fulfillment", Roussel remarks, "I only really knew the feeling of success when I used to sing to my own piano accompaniment and, more especially, through numerous impersonations which I did of actors or of anyone else. But there, at least, my success was enormous and unanimous"[8] The writings, too, are full of impersonators, from the understudy in *La Doublure* to the boy Bob Bucharessas (bouche à ressasse: mouth to repeat) who performed, ironically enough, at the "gala of the Incomparables" in *Impressions d'Afrique*:

"With extraordinary accomplishment and talent, a miracle of precociousness, the charming infant began a series of imitations which he accompanied with expressive gestures; the different sounds of a train getting up speed, the cries of domestic animals, a saw grating on a free-stone, the sharp pop of a champagne cork, the gurgling of liquid as it is poured out of a bottle, the fanfare of hunting horns, a violin solo and the plaintive notes of a cello, all these comprised an astounding repertoire which, to anyone who shut his eyes for a moment, afforded a complete illusion of reality."[9]

The trans-gendered impersonations within *Impressions d'Afrique*, of Carmichaël, who sings with a woman's voice, and of the king Talou, who insists on being taught to sing in the same style and performs at the gala in a wig of blond curls and a plunging blue dress, would no doubt no doubt have interested Duchamp, with his bearded Mona Lisa and his female alter ego Rrose Sélavy (under whose name many of his puns were published, many playing with the shift between masculine and feminine nouns in French). I have chosen these examples because, in their exaggerated forms, they perhaps make it easier to recognise the impersonation within Floyer's work. Although the examples just mentioned consist of men dressing as women, we would consider them less transvestites than female impersonators, the reason being, perhaps, that a transvestite would have us believe that he is actually a woman whereas a female impersonator plays on our understanding that this is a man pretending to be a woman (indeed, if we really believed that he was a woman, then the act would have in some important sense failed). Similarly, the sound of a train gathering speed is of less interest if we think that it is coming from a train rather than from the mouth of a four year old boy. The pleasure of impersonations derives from the fact that something is not what it is pretending to be, although it bears an obvious similarity to it.

So, perhaps we should think of the light switch in Floyer's work as an impersonation rather than an imitation, which is why the means of its production are so obvious within the space, the projector sitting on a plinth right before it. There are many other examples amongst Floyer's works: *Carousel* (1996), a record player which plays the sound of a slide projector moving through its carousel of slides, the circular movement in some ways mimicing it also; similarly, *Glass* (1997), a 7" clear vinyl record on which is recorded the tone produced by a finger moving around the rim of a glass. In this case, the stylus mimics the movement of the finger although once again there is no danger of it actually being mistaken for that original action. There's *Bucket* (1999) too, which consists of a bucket in which is placed a CD player and loudspeaker, clearly visible. The sound which emerges is that of a water drop as it hits the bottom of such a bucket, and so we are tempted to believe that this is the case (I bet you look up at the ceiling above) despite the fact that we can see what is actually producing the sound. Everything is visible, nothing hidden.

"The greater the accumulation of precise minutiae, of details of form and dimension, the more the object loses its depth. So this is an opacity without mystery, just as there is nothing behind the surfaces of a backcloth, no inside, no secret, no ulterior motive."[10]

We can see this, also, in another work, *Light* (1994), a slide projection installation which consists, so we are told, of four 35mm metal mask slides, four projectors, and a matt white sprayed light bulb on disconnected flex. The bulb hangs from the ceiling, as one would expect, the projectors mounted upon the surrounding walls, equidistant to the bulb, at the corners of an imaginary square, each projecting their little bulb-shaped piece of light at the white-painted object hanging between them. And so it glows, this radiant light within a darkened room (like Roussel's study perhaps, during his "crisis"?). But why is the room so dark if there hangs a light at its centre?

"It was only natural that these contorted shapes and numerous mechanisms doing nothing gave rise to the idea of an enigma, a cypher, a secret. Surrounding this machinery and inside it, there is a persistent night through which one senses that it is hidden. But this night is a kind of sun without rays or space; its radiance is cut down to fit these shapes, constituting their very being, and not their opening to visibility: a self-sufficient and enclosed sun."[11]

There is a trick, then we're shown how it's done. This is as true of Floyer's work as it is of Roussel's (who, after all, wrote that he'd always intended to explain how he'd created certain of his books). Roussel's constructions might seem phantasmagorical, Floyer's rather everyday in comparison, yet they seem to operate in a very similar

**Bucket** 1999
Bucket, CD, CD player, loudspeaker

**Helix**   2001
Helix template and found objects

way, in that the enjoyment we derive from them is dependent upon the play of impersonation and our role in recognising the deceit, such as it is:

"Now this chain of extraordinarily complex, ingenious and far-fetched elucidations seems so ludicrous and so disappointing that it is as if the mystery were still intact. But from now on it is a cleansed, eviscerated mystery that has become unnameable. The opacity no longer hides anything. It's like finding a locked drawer, and then a key, and the key opens the drawer impeccably à and the drawer is empty."[12]

What is interesting with *Light*, and also *Garbage Bag* (1996), which consists of a black refuse bag, tied full of air, is that they are objects which are to some extent impersonating themselves, rather than another object. Indeed, what is the difference between two things, seemingly identical, but where one is impersonating itself? What would be the difference between an ordinary bin bag and *Garbage Bag*, for example? Or what of Floyer's *Nail Biting Performance* at the Symphony Hall which takes place just before Stravinsky's *Rite of Spring*? In appearing on stage, biting her nails, Floyer impersonates a nervous performer, although that doesn't preclude the possibility of her actually being nervous. To approach such a question is dangerous. It is to ask what is the difference between art and non-art, and that is a question which has exercised a great many people over a great many years, and to no great effect. Let's think about it by thinking around it.

In 1999 Floyer produced two photographic works, *Half Empty* and *Half Full*, works which are obviously related.[13] In fact, they look identical, each showing what appears to be the same glass containing an amount of water which seems to occupy half its volume (obviously this is another of Floyer's works where the form is suggested by the title, a picture made from words). As the works are not shown side by side it is impossible to compare their visual similarity, although we have been told that the prints have been made from two different negatives (and so are different in the strict sense which Leibniz might have insisted upon). Yet it would be impossible for us, the viewer in the gallery, to tell them apart, or rather, to say which was which, which was half full, and which was half empty. It depends on how you look at it, is the response which the work seems to demand. What this work seems to suggest, therefore, is that two things which appear identical can have very different (in this case opposite) meanings.

We can find something similar in Jorge Luis Borges' extraordinary story, 'Pierre Menard, author of the *Quixote*'. A story which appears to be a work of literary criticism, 'Pierre

**Half Full** 1999
Colour photograph on aluminium
120 x 120cm

**Garbage Bag**  1996
Garbage bag, air, twist-tie

Menard...' looks at a work by the eponymous author found amongst his papers after his death. "This work, perhaps the most significant of our time, consists of the ninth and thirty-eighth chapters of the first part of *Don Quixote* and a fragment of chapter twenty-two." This is not merely some modern updating, as Borges makes clear:

"He did not want to compose another *Quixote* – which is easy – but the *Quixote* itself. Needless to say, he never contemplated a mechanical transcription of the original; he did not propose to copy it. His admirable intention was to produce a few pages which would coincide – word for word and line for line – with those of Miguel de Cervantes.[14] It is only through immense hard work – 'he multiplied draft upon draft, revised tenaciously and tore up thousands of manuscript pages' – that Menard is able to make his slow progress. Yet despite the difficulties inherent on such a task.

'Menards fragmentary *Quixote* is more subtle than Cervantes'. The latter, in a clumsy fashion, opposes to the fictions of chivalry the tawdry provincial reality of his country: Menard selects as his 'reality' the land of Carmen during the century of Lepanto and Lope de Vega...

Cervantes' text and Menard's are verbally identical, but the second is almost infinitely richer. (More ambiguous, his detractors will say, but ambiguity is richness.)"[15]

Menard's *Quixote* has no need of opposing the fictions of chivalry as Cervantes' book had long since rendered them obsolete; similarly, Cervantes would not have considered his the century of Lepanto and Lope de Vega, as it was simply the age in which he lived, and it was certainly not the land of Carmen, a nineteenth-century literary creation. Although they share the same words, these identical texts perform very different tasks, respond to very different intentions. In exploring the century of Lepanto and Lope de Vega, Menard is also exploring the century of Cervantes, and of his *Quixote*. Reference to this earlier *Quixote* is part of what Menard's work is about; logically, this cannot be the case for Cervantes'.

I think that we can consider Menard's *Quixote*, then, of possessing a degree of self-consciousness which separates it from that which it impersonates, and I think that we can extend this notion to the works of Floyer which we have considered also. As we mentioned earlier, impersonation depends upon the awareness that impersonation is taking place (as opposed to illusionism or imitation, which depends upon it being hidden) and at the risk of anthropomorphising the artworks, there is an undoubted self-consciousness at work here. That *Light* is impersonating a standard lightbulb is part of the work, just as it is when *Garbage Bag* is impersonating a garbage bag, or *Light Switch* a light switch. This is something which a "real" lightbulb, garbage bag or light switch – even within the same galleries – just couldn't do.

This self-consciousness is equal to an awareness of their own materiality, the supposed transparency of mimetic representation made visible to itself and to us. Consider *Light Bulb (Floor)* (1996) for example, or *Spot Light (Wall)* (1998), which both consist of an "ordinary" fitted and working lightbulb with a magnifying glass held just below it. The magnifying glass acts as a lens, projecting onto the floor, or wall, the manufacturer's name and the bulb's specification as it is printed on its surface, albeit reversed. "OSRAM", we might then be able to work out, "60W", or "PHILIPS" or whatever. If we attempted to read the text upon the bulb itself, by looking directly at it, we would see nothing, or rather we would see too much, too much light. We would see the light, so to speak, and not the bulb. Through a simple action, Floyer allows us to see the transparency (and opacity) of the bulb itself, a seeming inversion. It is like the shift between transparency and opacity which occurs in *Blind* (1997) where, at first, we cannot see the (roller) blind against the window even though that is all there is to see, and only become aware of it when the faint outline of the window-frame appears behind as the material blows in the breeze. The classical "window onto the world" which representation promised remains obscured; in becoming conscious of that which frames such a view, our ability to perceive is greatly improved. What we are looking at, to borrow a phrase from Arthur C Danto, is the "transfiguration of the commonplace"[16] It is art happening.

Ceal Floyer's work looks simple; often it looks as if there is nothing to see (although as Duchamp pithily remarked, one can look at seeing). Yet, as we have seen, these works can lead us in important directions, allowing us to consider the nature of representation, or the difference between art and non-art. We can accept this challenge; or we can simply smile to ourselves, and appreciate their "rightness" as artworks, however they happen.

## Notes

**1**    Quoted in Linda Dalrymple Henderson, *Duchamp in Context – Science and Technology in the Large Glass and Related Works*, Princeton University Press, Princeton 1998, p.51

**2**    A number of Duchamp's puns are included in (eds.) Michel Sanouillet and Elmer Peterson, *The Writings of Marcel Duchamp*, Da Capo Press, New York 1973. Given that Floyer's *Nail Biting Performance* takes place just before Stravinsky's *Rite of Spring*, it is perhaps appropriate to include also the following, translated by Elmer Peterson:

> Il faut dire:
> La crasse du tympan, et non le Sacre du Printemps.
> (One must say:
> Grease of eardrum and not Rite of Spring.)

**3**    Michel Foucault, *Death and the Labyrinth – The World of Raymond Roussel*, trans. Charles Ruas, Athlone Press, London 1987, p.11

**4**    Dr Pierre Janet, 'The Psychological Characteristics of Ecstasy' (1926), trans. John Harman, in (eds.) Alistair Brotchie et al, *Atlas Anthology 4: Raymond Roussel – Life, Death and Works* Atlas Press, London 1987, p.39

**5**    Alain Robbe-Grillet, 'Énigmes et transparence chez Raymond Roussel' (1963), trans. Barbara Wright as 'Riddles and Transparencies in Raymond Roussel', in *ibid.*, p.104

**6**    Raymond Roussel, 'Comment j'ai écrit certains de mes livres' (*c*.1931), trans. Trevor Winkfield as 'How I Wrote Certain of my Books' in (ed. and trans). Trevor Winkfield, *How I Wrote Certain of my Books*, Exact Change, Boston 1995, p.3

**7**    Quoted in Mark Ford, *Raymond Roussel and the Republic of Dreams*, Faber & Faber, London 2000, p.96. The first major study of Roussel's life and work in English, this book is recommended to anyone with an interest in Roussel or, indeed, the development of the avant-garde in the twentieth century.

**8**    *How I Wrote Certain of my Books*, p.28

**9**    Raymond Roussel, *Impressions d'Afrique* (1910) trans. Lindy Foord and Rayner Heppenstall as *Impressions of Africa*, John Calder, London 1983, pp.32–3

**10**    'Riddles and Transparencies in Raymond Roussel', p.101

**11**    *Death and the Labyrinth – The World of Raymond Roussel*, p.65

**12** 'Riddles and Transparencies in Raymond Roussel', p.102

**13** Of course, these works also have a relationship with a work by another artist, Michael Craig-Martin. In 1974, Craig-Martin exhibited *An Oak Tree* (1973) at the Rowan Gallery, London, a work which has become extremely important to British conceptualism, and around which one might usefully base a discussion of the imitation or impersonation of objects by other objects (although that is for some other time). To look at, the work consists of a glass shelf, supported high upon a wall by two chrome brackets, like an untouchable bathroom shelf. Upon the shelf sits a glass tumbler, which contains some water. A sheet of paper also within the gallery contains a 'fake' interrogation of the artist which goes some way to explaining the title of the work:

> **Q**. To begin with could you describe this work?
> **A**. Yes, of course. What I've done is change a glass of water into a full-grown oak tree without altering the accidents of the glass of water.
> **Q**. The accidents?
> **A**. Yes. The colour, feel, weight, size.
> **Q**. Haven't you simply called this glass of water an oak tree?
> **A**. Absolutely not. It is not a glass of water anymore. I have changed its actual substance. It would no longer be accurate to call it a glass of water. One could call it anything one wished but that would not alter the fact that it is an oak tree…
> **Q**. Do you consider that changing the glass of water into an oak tree constitutes an artwork?
> **A**. Yes.

Quoted from Tony Godfrey, *Conceptual Art*, Phaidon, London 1998, p.248

**14** Jorge Luis Borges, *Labyrinths*, Penguin Books, Harmondsworth 1970, pp.65 – 6

**15** *Ibid.*, pp.68 – 9

**16** Arthur C. Danto, *The Transfiguration of the Commonplace*, Harvard University Press, Cambridge, Massachusetts 1981. Danto's book is a far more rigorous and intelligent exploration into the defining of "the work of art" than I have been able to make in this essay (than I am able to make, period). Unsurprisingly, one of the many works which catches his attention is the fragmentary manuscript of M. Menard.

overleaf:
**Blind** 1997
VHS video loop without sound

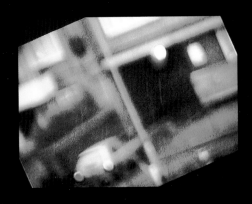

**Downpour** 2001
DVD projection

**Mousehole** 1994
Ink on DIN A4 paper

```
        KWIKSAVE  MOSELEY
        SOMERFIELD STORES LTD
        BRISTOL   BS14 0TJ


BOTTLE BRUSH          0.69
SKIMMED              0.27
50 E/LOPES           0.99
WRITING PAD          0.89
PAPER PLATES         0.99
DES COCONUT          0.39
POLO MINTS           0.19
SAXA SALT            0.55
SINGLE CREAM         0.42
PHILADELPHIA         1.09
SF LARD              0.12
ANDREX WHITE         1.06
DOVE BAR             1.29
CIF ORIG             1.09
ELECT. BULBS         0.99
COD PORTIONS         2.69
PLAIN FLOUR          0.42
COOK IN SCE          0.74
HARTLEY SOUP         0.19
L/GRAIN RICE         1.15
MAYONNAISE           1.29
BICARB SODA          0.45
SF BABY TALC         0.49
ICING SUGAR          0.55
PAMPERS              5.65
REG TISSUES          1.48
SHAVING FOAM         1.19
GLOSS PAINT          2.17
LILLETS              1.38
NIVEA CREME          1.33
CLGT T/PASTE         1.49
FIRE LIGHTER         0.35
WASHING PWDR         0.94
BASICS BIN           0.99
MILK OF MAG          1.99
PARACETAMOL          0.19
SUBTOTAL            38.14

CASH               40.00
CHANGE              1.86

  NO. OF ITEMS       36

  VAT NUMBER 107 4212 12
REC    DATE   TIME  MACH TERM
4648 08.02.01 09:57 5542 0002
```

**Monochrome Till Receipt (White)**  2001

Ink on paper on wall

**Crawl and Scroll**   2001
DVD projection

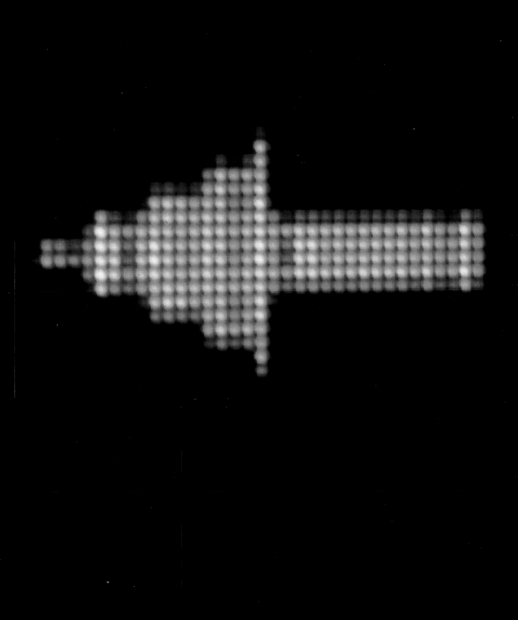

**1968**
Born in Karachi, Pakistan

**1991–94**
BA Goldsmiths College, London

Lives and works in London

**1997**
Awarded Philip Morris Scholarship, Künstlerhaus
Bethanien, Berlin

**Solo exhibitions**

**1995**
Picture Gallery, Science Museum, London

**1996**
Galleria Primo Piano, Rome (part of *Artisti britannici
a Roma*, The British Council)

Tramway Project Room, Glasgow

Anthony Wilkinson Fine Art, London

Gavin Brown's enterprise, New York

**1997**
Galleria Gianluca Collica, Catania, Sicily

City Racing, London

Herzliya Museum of Art, Tel Aviv

Lisson Gallery, London

Galleria Primo Piano, Rome

**1998**
Künstlerhaus Bethanien, Berlin (exh. cat)

**1999**
Casey Kaplan, New York

Kunsthalle Bern, Switzerland

**2000**
Pinksummer, Genoa

**2001**
Ikon Gallery, Birmingham

Institute of Visual Arts, Milwaukee

CCA, Berkeley

**Group exhibitions**

**1992**
*Hit & Run*, Tufton Street, London

**1993**
*Infanta of Castile at Goldhawk Road*, London

*Fast Surface*, Chisenhale Gallery, London

**1994**
*Fast Forward*, Institute of Contemporary Art, London
(ICA Live Arts commission)

*Making Mischief*, St. James' Street, London

**1995**
*Freddy Contreras/Ceal Floyer*, The Showroom, London

*General Release: Young British Artists at Scuola
di San Pasquale*, Venice Biennale

*Just Do It*, Cubitt Gallery, London

*4th Istanbul Biennale*, Turkey

*British Art Show 4*, Manchester/Edinburgh/Cardiff

*Five Artists*, Frith Street Gallery, London

**1996**
*Oporto's Festival of Contemporary Art*, Portugal

*Viper*, Bank TV, London & Manchester

**1996–97**
*Life/Live*, Musée d'Art Moderne de la Ville de Paris;
Centro Cultural de Belem, Lisbon

**1997**

*Light*, Richard Salmon Fine Art, London (toured to Spacex, Exeter)

*Belladonna*, Institute of Contemporary Art, London

*Treasure Island*, Centro de Art Moderna/Calouste Gulbenkian Foundation, Lisbon

*Sentimental Education*, Cabinet Gallery, London

*Urban Legends – London*, Staatliche Kunsthalle Baden-Baden

*You Are Here*, Royal College of Art, London

*I Luoghi Ritrovati*, Centro Civico Per L'Arte Contemporanea La Grancia Serre di Rapolano, Siena

*Material Culture: the object in British art in the 80s and 90s*, Hayward Gallery, London

*Projects*, Irish Museum of Modern Art

*Pictura Britannica*, Museum of Contemporary Art, Sydney (toured to Art Gallery of South Australia, Adelaide; City Gallery, Wellington)

**1998**

*Genius loci*, Kunsthalle Bern

*Martin Creed, Ceal Floyer, John Frankland*, Delfina Studios, London

*Dimensions variable*, British Council touring exhibition

*Sunday*, Cabinet Gallery, London

*Seamless*, De Appel Foundation, Amsterdam

*In the Meantime*, Galeria Estrany-de la Moto, Barcelona

*Real/Life – New British Art 1998–1999*, Tochigi Prefectural Museum of Fine Arts (toured to Fukuoka City Art Museum; Hiroshima City Museum of Contemporary Art; Tokyo Museum of Contemporary Art; Ashiya City Museum of Art and History)

*Drawing Itself*, London Institute Gallery

*Then and Now*, Lisson Gallery, London

*In the meantime*, Galeria Estrany De La Mota, Barcelona

*New Art from Britain*, Kunstraum Innsbruck, Innsbruck, Germany

*Every Day*, 11th Biennale of Sydney

*Malos Habitos*, Soledad Lorenzo, Madrid

*Triennale der Kleinplastik*, Stuttgart

*Thinking Aloud*, South Bank Centre touring exhibition curated by Richard Wentworth: Kettles Yard, Cambridge; Cornerhouse, Manchester; Camden Arts Centre, London

*minimalisms*, Akademie der Künste, Berlin

*Richard Wentworth & Ceal Floyer*, Galerie Carlos Poy, Barcelona

**1999**

*Looking at Ourselves: Works by Women Artists from the Logan Collection*, MoMA, San Fransisco

*Richard Wentworth & Ceal Floyer*, Galeria Rafael Ortiz, Seville

*On Your Own Time*, P.S.1 Contemporary Art Centre, New York

*This Other World of Ours*, TV Gallery, Moscow

*Luminous Mischief*, Yokohama Portside Gallery, Kanagawa, Japan

*Mirror's Edge*, Bild Museet, Umeå, Sweden (toured to Vancouver Art Gallery, Canada; Castello di Rivoli, Torino; Tramway, Glasgow)

*Peace*, Museum für Gegenwarts Kunst, Zurich

*Trace*, International Exhibition, Tate Gallery Liverpool, Liverpool Biennale

*Dimensions Variable*, The Ludwig Museum Budapest – Museum of Contemporary Art, Budapest

**2000**

*Edit*, Badischer Kunstverein, Karlsruhe

*Crossroads: Artists in Berlin*, Communidad de Madrid, Madrid

*Quotidiana*, Castello di Rivoli, Turin

*Drive*, Govett-Brewster Art Gallery, New Plymouth, New Zealand

*Making Time: Considering Time as a Material in Contemporary Video & Film*, Palm Beach Institute of Contemporary Art, Palm Beach, Florida, U.S

*Extra Ordinary*, James Cohan Gallery, New York

*Film/Video Works – Lisson Gallery at 9 Keane Street*, Lisson Gallery, London

*A Shot in the Head*, Lisson Gallery, London

**2001**

*City Racing 1988 – 1998: a partial account*, Institute of Contemporary Art, London

## Screenings

**1996**

*The Meaning of Life (Part II),* CCA, Glasgow; Art Nolde, Stockholm

*Such is Life*, Serpentine Gallery Bookshop, London

**1999**

*Fourth Wall – Waiting*, Public Art Development Trust in association with the Royal National Theatre, South Bank, London

## Bibliography

### Books and Catalogues

**1994**

*The City of Dreadful Night* artist's project, Rear Window at Atlantis Lower Gallery, London

**1995**

*Freddy Contreras/Ceal Floyer* (exh. cat) The Showroom, London

Smith's Magazine (artist's page), Goldsmiths College, London

*General Release: Young British Artists at Scuola di San Pasquale* (artist's page/exh. cat) British Council

*Orientation: The Vision of Art in a Paradoxical World* (exh. cat) 4th Istanbul Biennale

**1996**

*The British Art Show 4* (exh. cat) South Bank Centre – National Touring Exhibitions

untitled artists' book, published by Imprint 93, London

*Artisti britannici a Roma* (exh. cat), British Council

*Slide Show* (exh. cat), Tramway Project Room, Glasgow

*Life/Live* (exh. cat), Musée d'Art Moderne de la Ville de Paris

**1997**

*Treasure Island* (exh. cat), Calouste Gulbenkian Foundation

*Urban Legends – London* (exh. cat), Staatliche Kunsthalle, Baden-Baden

*You Are Here* (exh. cat), Royal College of Art, London

*Projects* (exh. cat), Irish Museum of Modern Art, Dublin Artist pages, Hyperfoto, No.3– 4

*Dimensions Variable*, British Council, London

**1998**

*Seamless*, De Appel Foundation, Amsterdam

*Real/Life:New British Art*, The Asahi Shimbun, Japan

*Drawing itself*, London Institute Gallery

*Every Day*, 11th Biennale of Sydney, Sydney (exh. cat)

*Zeitgenossische Skulptur Europa Africa*, 7 Triennale der Kleinplastik 1998, Germany (exh. cat)

*Cream*, portable exhibition in a book, curated by Carlos Basualso, Francesco Bonami, Dan Cameron, Okuwui Enwezor, Matthew Higgs, Hou Hanru, Susan Kandel, Rosa Martinez, Åsa Nacking and Hans Ulrich Obrist, Phaidon, London

**1999**

*Ceal Floyer*, Kunsthalle Bern (exh. cat)

*Peace*, Museum Fur Gegenwarts Kunst, Zurich (exh. cat)

**2000**

*Quotidiana*, Castello di Rivoli, Turin (exh. cat)

*Edit*, Badischer Kunstverein, Karlsruhe

*Crossroads, Artists in Berlin*, Sala de Exposiciones de Plaza de Espagna, Communidad de Madrid, Madrid

**Selected Articles And Reviews**

**1993**

David Lillington, 'The Infanta of Castile', *Time Out*, London, 2–9 June

Margaret Garlake, 'From the Infanta to the Lemon', *Art Monthly*, No. 168, July–August

**1994**

Tania Guha, 'Making Mischief', *Time Out*, London, 7–14 December

David Barrett, 'Making Mischief', *Art Monthly*, No. 182, December/January

Rob Kessler, 'City of Dreadful Night', *Untitled*, No. 7

Brian Muller, 'A Real Art', *Art Line*, Vol. 6, No. 2, Winter

**1995**

Geraldine Norman, 'Turning the Tide in Venice', *The Independent on Sunday*, 12 March

Marianne Macdonald, 'Removal Art…', *The Independent*, 25 April

Richard Cork, 'Mourning a little death in Venice', *The Times*, 14 June

William Feaver, 'Don't Look Now,' *The Observer Review*, 18 June

Sotiris Kyriacou, 'Ceal Floyer/Freddy Contreras', *Art Monthly*, No.187, June

Margaret Garlake, 'Adrift in Venice', *Art Monthly*, No.188, July/August

Michael Archer, 'Home and Away', *Art Monthly*, No. 188, July/August

**1996**

Michael Archer, 'Reconsidering Conceptual Art', *Art Monthly*, No. 193, February

James Hall, 'The British Art Show 4', *Art Forum*, XXXIV, No.214, June

David Barrett, 'Playing Dumb: David Barrett on Ceal Floyer', *Art Monthly*, No. 193, February

David Barrett, 'Kiss This', *Art Monthly*, No. 195, April

Patricia Bickers, 'The Young Devils', *Art Press*, No. 214, June

Paul Welsh, 'Slide Show', *Art Review*, June

Andrew Wilson, 'Life/Live', *Art Monthly*, No. 201, November

Michael Newman, 'Conceptual Art from the 1960s to the 1990s: An unfinished project?', *Museum Journal*

**1997**

Brian Muller 'Ceal Floyer', *Flash Art*, May – June

Carl Freedman, 'Generation W(eird)', *The Guardian*, London, 27 May

Godfrey Worsdale, 'Soundings: Ceal Floyer' *Artist's Newsletter*, June 1997

David Batchelor, Carl Freedman, 'Living in a material world', *Frieze*, Issue 53, June, July, August

Michael Archer, 'Ceal Floyer, City Racing', *Art Monthly*, June

Courtney Kidd, 'Pictura Britannica', *Art Monthly,* Issue 37, November – December

Brian Muller, 'Ceal Floyer: Seeing the light', *Contemporary Visual Arts*, Issue 16

Matthew Collings, 'From Sydney to Stussy City, *Modern Painters*, vol.10, No 4

**1998**

David Green, 'Minimal interventions', *Contemporary Visual Arts*, Issue 17

'Ceal Floyer: Contact Print 1 – 24', artist collaboration commissioned for *Contemporary Visual Arts*, commentary by Maite Lorés, Issue 21

David Musgrave, 'The Last Show', *Art Monthly*, No. 222, 98 – 99

**1999**

Nick de Ville, 'Unfinished Business', *Contemporary Visual Arts*, Issue 22

David Barrett, 'Richard Wentworth's Thinking Aloud', *Frieze*, Issue 45

Rebecca Fortnum*,* 'A slight intervention on the work of Elizabeth Wright and Ceal Floyer', *Make*, no.83, March

Rene Ammann, 'Ceal Floyer', *Artforum International*, September

Lisa Liebmann and Brooks Adams, 'A Summer Place', *Art in America*, June

Howard Halle, 'Ceal Floyer', *Time Out* New York, 30 September – 7 October, Issue 210

'La Biennale di Liverpool: Trace', *Flash Art*, (Ital.), Oct ober – November

Caoimhin Mac Giolla Leith 'Liverpool Biennale Of Contemporary Art'

*Art Forum International* / Special Issue 'Best of the '90s', December

Valerie Reardon, Trace, *Art Monthly,* Nr. 231, November

'Mirror's Edge', *Flash Art*, November – December

**2000**

C.B., 'Lisson Video Show', *Flash Art International*, summer

Tanya Gorucheva, 'This Other World of Ours', *Flash Art*, January – February

Nico Israel, 'Ceal Floyer', *Artforum*, February

Helena Kontova, 'Mirror's Edge, An Interview with Curator Okwui Enwezor', *Flash Art*, March – April

Lars O Ericsson, 'Mirror's Edge', *Art Forum*, Summer

Charles Darwent, 'Lisson Gallery @ 9 Kean Street', *Metro*, 18 April

Rachel Campbell-Johnston, 'State of the art video', *The Times*, 3 May Polly Staple, 'Video Show House', *Art Monthly*, July – August

Tony Godfrey, London, 'Roni Horn, Craigie Horsfield, and contemporary artists' video', *Burlington Magazine*, July

Ina Blom, 'White Mischief', *nu: The Nordic Art Review*, vol.II, No. 5/00k

Phillipe Mathonnet*,* 'Avec trois fois rien, Ceal Floyer cherche a suggerer infiniment plus', *Le Temps,* Geneva, November

# Ceal Floyer

8 February – 25 March 2001
Ikon Gallery, Birmingham

Exhibition curated by Jonathan Watkins assisted by Kaye Winwood.

© Ikon Gallery, the artist and authors
All rights reserved. No part of this book
may be used or reproduced in any
manner without written permission from
the publisher, except in the context
of reviews. The publisher has made
every effort to contact all copyright
holders. If proper acknowledgement
has not been made, we ask copyright
holders to contact the publisher.
All works courtesy of Lisson Gallery,
London and Casey Kaplan, New York.

Ikon Gallery
1 Oozells Square
Brindleyplace
Birmingham, B1 2HS
t: +44 (0)121 248 0708
f: +44 (0)121 248 0709
email: art@ikon-gallery.co.uk
http://www.ikon-gallery.co.uk
Registered charity no: 528892

Edited by Jonathan Watkins
Designed by Herman Lelie
Typeset by Stefania Bonelli
Photography by Gary Kirkham and
Hugo Glendinning
Printed by PJ Print
Distributed by Cornerhouse Publications
70 Oxford Street, Manchester, M1 5NH
publications@cornerhouse.org
t: +44 (0)161 200 1503
f: +44 (0)161 200 1504

Ikon Staff

Philip Duckworth
*Visitor Assistant*
Katya Garcia-Anton
*Curator (Gallery)*
Celine Haran
*Deputy Director*
Marcus Herron
*Facilities Technician IT/AV*
Gurminder Kenth
*Visitor Assitant*
Deborah Kermode
*Curator (Offsite)*
Helen Juffs
*Gallery Facilities Manager*
James Langdon
*Marketing Assistant*
Chris Maggs
*Facilities Technician*
Nikki Matthews
*Education Assistant*
John Paul Mc Aree
*Programme Assistant*
Gill Nicol
*Curator (Education and Interpretation)*
Kristin Onions
*Visitor Assistant*
Eloise Saunders
*Visitor Assistant*
Lucy Stevens
*Marketing Manager*
Dianne Tanner
*Finance Manager*
Andrew Tims
*Education Assistant*
Sharon Townsend
*PA/Office Coordinator*
Andy Turner
*Visitor Assistant*
Jean Virgo
*Visitor Assistant*
Jonathan Watkins
*Director*
Kaye Winwood
*Exhibitions Coordinator*

## Acknowledgments

Thanks to the following individuals
for their support:

Lolly Batty, Rory Conquest,
Thomas Demand, Nicholas Logsdail,
Stephen Maddock, Silke Otto-Knapp,
Andreas Schimanski, Lisa Rosendahl,
Joseph Swensen

Exhibition supported by The Henry
Moore Foundation

Ikon gratefully acknowledges financial
assistance from The Arts Council of
England, Birmingham City Council and
West Midlands Arts

Cover:
**Nail Biting Performance**
7 February 2001
Symphony Hall, Birmingham

ISBN 0 907594 71 9